White Is Bright When She See The Light

Tonya Massenburg

To order additional copies of this book, contact:
Xlibris
844-714-8691
www.Xlibris.com
Orders@Xlibris.com

ISBN: Softcover   978-1-6641-6447-5
       Hardcover   978-1-6641-6448-2
       EBook   978-1-6641-6446-8

Print information available on the last page

Rev. date: 03/23/2021

Contents

Poem 1

The Eye,

Invision the winning wealth
Of your humble health
Sworn in and held by
One's tutelage belt

Poem 2.
White Power

You knocking hard
But she loves living large
And how your manhood
Take charge!
Yea, love it so much
Wanna hug it
Never plan to mug it!

Poem 3.

Heavenly Explosion

Do not cocktail the cottontail
Why you own the bed and train rails,
With you I cannot lose
Because I am moved
By your blue eyed clues
Now, isn't that good news?

Poem 4.

100% LOVER

A viking that is like no other
That bill you feel will
Seal the kill
Fluctuating sensation
Horsing around
From sun up to sun down
Although, she think of you
Like a brother
LK37600912A this serial number
Is my 100% lover

Poem 5.
Rudiments of the gov't

The rudiments are not red
She shed the feathers
From her dreads
Resembling hot creamy alfredo
Stooping too sweet n low
Game planning the afro
Because he is labeled as
A true Jethro starring
In the freeze please show
In the brothel he is their hero
But to the latter he is a zero
Unloved due to a pink show

Poem 6.

COLT 45 AND JIVE

Colt 45 and jive
Are not alive
In a state of mind
so bewildered
And left behind
Goody fruit and sickles
Has taste buds for lemon lime

Poem 7.

SEAL THE KILL

What ye fail to realize
Is HE will kill for your eyes
When that is not enough
To heal your stuff
They will not know the price shonuff
Is like walking in the cold air of winter
Without ear muffs
Let the bear paws
Drive the bus
He is a Royal Crown bae
A si a si a we can do this today

PHOTO GALLERY

Printed in the United States
by Baker & Taylor Publisher Services